SUMMARY
of Daniel Kahneman's
THINKING, FAST AND SLOW

by SUMOREADS

TABLE OF CONTENTS

Key Takeaway: Two Systems drive human thoughts and actions.

Take: Fast thinking is automatic and effortless. Slow thinking is deliberate and mentally exerting.

Key Takeaway: Overreliance on System 1 fosters irrationality and lazy thinking.

Key Takeaway: Hunger, self-control, and mental fatigue deplete System 2.

Key Takeaway: You can't be too sure of the reasons for your choices.

Key Takeaway: The human mind favors plausibility over probability, certainty over doubt.

Key Takeaway: Use individual cases, not statistics, to teach or spur action.

Key Takeaway: Causal thinking undermines ability to accurately evaluate random events.

Key Takeaway: Base rates make for better predictions than stereotype or similarity judgments.

Key Takeaway: Mobilize System 2 to correct intuitive guesses.

Key Takeaway: Extreme performance regresses to the mean over time, and that's all there is to it.

Key Takeaway: Confidence reflects the coherence, not the accuracy of the story.

Key Takeaway: An easily explainable past gives the illusion of an easily predictable future.

Key Takeaway: Simple algorithms do better than expert judgments in making predictions.

Key Takeaway: It takes practice in a stable, regular environment to acquire reliable intuition.

Key Takeaway: People are instinctively loss averse.

Key Takeaway: The remembering self dominates the experiencing self.

Key Takeaway: The peak and the end influence the memory of experiences.

EXECUTIVE SUMMARY

In his book *Thinking, Fast and Slow*, Daniel Kahneman explains how two fictitious mental systems influence thought processes, choices, and actions. He explores the heuristics, or assumptions, that create muddled thinking and demonstrates that the human mind is predictably irrational. He argues that only when individuals slow down, recognize the cognitive biases that influence their thought process, and rationalize their feelings and impressions can they hope to make more consistent judgments.

Kahneman points out that one mental system, which he dubs System 1, is in charge of the fast, automatic, and intuitive thinking that governs simple and routine tasks. It uses simple rules of thumb that often bias its impressions, feelings, and inclinations. The other system, which he labels System 2, is in charge of the slow, deliberate, and rational thinking that is usually mobilized to solve complex problems and complete difficult tasks. System 2 is the "unbeliever," the inner skeptic.

Human decisions, Kahneman argues, tend to be inconsistent because the lazy System 2 often endorses the irrational intuitive guesses made by System 1. It takes deliberate effort to consider options broadly and comprehensively and make rational decisions, but System 2 is biased toward the path of least effort.

INTRODUCTION

You can't tell how you got most of the intuitions and impressions that guide your experience because they are involuntary and outside of conscious reach. The loosely defined rules, or heuristics, that you use to make sense of the world around you cause predictable errors in judgment because they are not based on deliberate or rational thought.

Intuitions about the characters and behaviors of people, for example, are heavily biased by cultural stereotypes. People overly rely on resemblance and available information to make predictions and judge possibilities, even when a quick consideration of statistics would make for better judgment.

PART 1:
TWO SYSTEMS

Chapter 1: The Characters of the Story

The human mind uses two systems to make judgments, predictions, and solutions. System 1, which is quick and automatic, requires almost no effort. System 2, which is slow and deliberate, requires mental exertion, experience, and concentration. People think their beliefs and choices are conscious products of System 2, but it is the automatic impressions and feelings of System 1 that lead to most of these beliefs and choices.

The operations of System 1 give you an instant answer to a simple problem like 1+1. They enable you to instantly recognize objects, sentences, and facial expressions—often through learned skills and associations and experience. In contrast, the operations of System 2 require effort. It takes attention and effort to fill out forms, make complex arguments, or find specific objects in a group of many.

Both systems are intricately connected. System 1 is the source of the intuitions and feelings that System 2 turns into voluntary action or beliefs. System 1 calls for the additional attention and the conscious deliberation of System 2 when it encounters a puzzle or a complex problem for which a judgment or solution is not immediately obvious.

The automatic operations of System 1 make errors in judgment hard to detect.

Chapter 2: Attention and Effort

System 1 doesn't require much effort because it only considers simple relations and manages routine tasks. System 2 considers rules, combines ideas, makes comparisons and deliberate choices, and, consequently, requires more attention and effort and uses more energy.

Chapter 3: The Lazy Controller

Most of the activities coordinated by System 2—driving on a highway, reading a newspaper, having social conversations—take little effort and exert no strain on the mind. When you combine effortful activities, each activity competes for the same resources. The brain limits the effort exerted on one activity for the other activity to be successfully completed. Deliberate control of attention takes effort too, so it can take away from concentration.

System 2 controls thoughts and behavior. However, when you are fully engaged—when System 2 is occupied—System 1 influences your behavior and leans towards easy choices. When System 2 is depleted—by mentally tasking work, alcohol, sleeplessness—your self-control diminishes.

System 2 quickly endorses the intuitive suggestions made by System 1. It makes little effort to check their accuracy, or to slow down and check memory or rules of logic. Overriding intuition takes effort, which many people avoid, so intuitive errors easily become cognitive errors. People who don't invest the extra effort to check their intuitions overly rely on System 1 and tend to be impulsive.

Chapter 4: The Associative Machine

Conscious and subconscious exposure to words, images, and ideas "primes" you to think about and anticipate similar ideas. If you hear the word "laundry", for example, you are more likely to fill the missing letters in "s_ _p" with "oa" than "ou."

Ideas invariably influence your action, and your feelings catch up with your actions, even when you are not consciously aware. Exposure to images of classrooms primes an undecided voter so that he is more likely to vote in favor of increased school funding. If you nod as you listen to a message, you are more likely to agree with its content.

Chapter 5: Cognitive Ease

System 1 automatically assesses your body and environment whenever you are conscious. If everything is going well—if things look and feel familiar, effortless, and good—it registers cognitive ease. If there's a problem, it registers cognitive strain and mobilizes System 2. Judgments based on cognitive ease and strain are bound to be biased because the lazy brain often assumes that things that feel familiar and effortless—including repeated ideas, easy fonts and rhymes—are true.

"*A reliable way to make people believe in falsehoods is frequent repetition, because familiarity is not easily distinguished from truth*" (p. 62).

Chapter 6: Norms, Surprises, and Causes

System 1 links patterns to make sense of reality. It processes environmental cues, assigns intentions, and anticipates causalities, even where there are none. Assigning causes to random events helps one make sense of a chaotic world.

System 1 links ideas and events that occur at the same time to determine what is normal and what isn't. A rare occurrence is less surprising when encountered the second time because System 1 has already assigned some normalcy to it.

Chapter 7: A Machine for Jumping to Conclusions

To save time and effort, System 1 assesses what is familiar and draws near-instant conclusions from cues. It uses context and the memory of recent events to resolve ambiguity and guess the right solution. If a friend informs you that she's going to the bank, what comes to mind is money and bank tellers, not a river bank, because you go to the former more than the latter. If the cue is significantly ambiguous, System 2 is mobilized.

System 1 is biased toward jumping into conclusions and believing. It looks for confirmations of ideas it is exposed to and makes guesses that fit its impressions. If the guess or story it makes is coherent, the quality of the data it draws from is irrelevant. If information is scarce, System 1 will jump to the first conclusion that makes sense. If contradictory information comes up, System 1 will either ignore it or defend its earlier position.

System 2 brings in the questions and the doubts. However, since System 2 is lazy, it often accepts the impressions made by System 1, even when they are wrong, because it's easier to accept than question. When you are exhausted, you are more likely to be persuaded by faulty arguments because System 2, whose role is to unbelieve, is depleted.

Chapter 8: How Judgments Happen

System 1 makes rapid assessments of situations to make snap intuitive judgments. System 2 considers questions raised internally or externally and searches memory and knowledge base for answers. People can judge trustworthiness and leadership ability from physical appearance because System 1 is prone to matching. It makes little regard to the congruency of the traits it matches. It takes the more intentional and effortful operations of System 2 to assess the variables that actually determine competence.

System 1 can easily guess averages and gauge intensity, but it can't make computations—it can't guess actual sizes and numbers of things.

Chapter 9: Answering an Easier Question

If a question is complex and System 1 can't come up with a solution fast enough, it creates a substitute question—one that is adequate and related to the original question—which it answers instead. Substitution enables System 1 to simplify and answer impossible questions such as questions of probability, which it can't answer without statistics. Asked to judge how much should money should be dedicated to the conservation of an endangered species, you will likely substitute the computation of statistics needed to give an objective answer with your feelings about an endangered species.

System 1 comes up answers that match the intensity of your feelings. The lazy system 2 hardly notices when you don't answer the original question; it endorses System 1's answers by default. In this way, emotional attitudes determine most judgments.

PART 2:
HEURISTICS AND BIASES

Chapter 10: The Law of Small Numbers

While System 1 is good at linking patterns to make intuitive guesses, it struggles to accommodate statistical facts in its snap judgments. It often draws quick conclusions from the content of a message without considering the sample size or reliability of the data.

Small samples are prone to errors. Most people know this, but statistical facts are difficult to internalize. It's easy, for example, to conclude that an investment banker who makes remarkable returns for two consecutive years is exceptionally skilled. Even when you know two years is too short a period to reliably draw such a conclusion.

"If you follow your intuition, you will more often than not err by misclassifying a random event as systematic. We are far too willing to reject the belief that much of what we see in life is random" (p. 117).

Chapter 11: Anchors

When you are exposed to either relevant or irrelevant information before solving a problem, you are likely to use that information as a reference or anchor to evaluate the quantity or value of the solution. The price listed on a property, for example, may not reflect its value, but you will likely use the price to estimate the property's value.

Activating System 2 by trying to think the opposite can undermine the effect of the anchor. You are likely to stay closer to the anchor if System 2 is depleted—if you are tired or if you are actively solving other problems.

Chapter 12: The Science of Availability

The mind judges the frequency of events by the ease with which it retrieves instances of the event in question. If you have to judge the probability of an event—say, rates of divorce among elderly couples or your level of competence—your estimate will be high if you find it easy to retrieve instances of these events. The instances don't have to be many for retrieval to be easy. In fact, a few instances that are easy to retrieve influence a higher estimate than many instances that are hard to retrieve. Instances that are dramatic, high-profile, emotional, or that personally affect you are easy to retrieve.

You can only overcome availability bias if you question your reliance on the instances you retrieve from memory. Making deliberate effort to assess the quality of the information you have activates System 2, which brings the vigilance that guards against availability bias.

Chapter 13: Availability, Emotion, and Risk

Your perception of reality is influenced by the prevalence and emotional charge of the messages you are exposed to. Since media coverage is biased toward novel and emotional occurrences (such as ghastly or accidental deaths) you are more likely to overestimate their occurrence and underestimate the occurrence of common underreported incidences, such as deaths by disease.

Incidences that evoke fear are easy to retrieve, the occurrence of which is easy to overestimate. How strongly you feel about something has a significant effect on how you remember it and how you assess its risks and benefits.

Chapter 14: Tom W's Specialty

System 1 automatically links patterns and associates them with stereotypes. It assesses how similar or how representative an object is of its class and neglects other factors, such as probability and accuracy of the description. To guess the specialty of a graduate student from a personality sketch, people rely less on proportions of course enrollment and more on personality description.

Mental exercises that mobilize System 2—such as focusing, self-monitoring and self-questioning—improve a person's ability to make predictions. Irrelevant or untrustworthy information easily sways System 1 because in its rush to make quick judgments, it believes what it sees is all there is.

Chapter 15: Linda: Less is More

Most people would guess that Linda, a fictitious woman who has a philosophy major and is concerned about discrimination and social justice, is more of a feminist bank teller than a bank teller. Intuitively, it is not obvious that the specification lowers probability: the probability of Linda being a bank teller is higher than that of her being a feminist bank teller.

Statisticians are as likely to err as lay people because their often-illogical and easily impressionable System 1 is as active, and the doubting System 2 is often in inattentive.

Chapter 16: Causes Trump Statistics

System 1 constructs a representation of the typical member of a population and uses it to make judgments of other members. If facts contradict this interpretation, it finds it easier to ignore them. A coherent story invariably beats statistics.

In an experiment that shows how responsibility is diluted in a crowd, only 27 percent of the participants rushed to help a choking victim. When psychology students are shown the results of the experiment along with brief, non-informative interviews of the participants, they still judge most of the participants as likely to help. Their view of the participants as nice, decent people overwhelms their ability to process the dire statistics.

Chapter 17: Regression to the Mean

Improvement often follows poor performance, and deterioration often follows good performance, regardless of external influence. Because success is influenced by both talent and luck, subsequent performance is likely to move closer to the average as luck improves or fades. In the absence of other information, it should be expected that a very good start should be followed by a high regression to the mean.

Causal stories that explain this change are plausible and convincing (because the human mind, with its associative memory. favors causal interpretations), but are hardly ever backed by evidence.

Chapter 18: Taming Intuitive Predictions

System 1 substitutes the difficult task of making a future prediction for the easier task of assessing current performance. If it finds coherence in its current assessment—if things feel right—it naturally overestimates and puts too much confidence in its prediction. An interviewee who comes off as brilliant during an interview, for example, is likely to be judged as competent in the role she is interviewing for even though her resume shows she has no experience.

Predictions that do not accommodate regression to the mean are biased and distanced from actual performance. To make an accurate prediction, start with a guess, then list the factors you would use to make a prediction. Give each of the factors a value, and then use these values to move your guess closer to the average of the class or category of the event you are considering.

PART 3: OVERCONFIDENCE

Chapter 19: The Illusion of Understanding

The human mind is strongly biased toward good stories, irrespective of their completeness or accuracy. If information is limited, the mind will fill the missing pieces with the explanations that make most sense. It overestimates the predictability of events to do away with the anxiety that comes with uncertainty.

Biographic writers covering iconic figures and companies tap into this need for certainty. By distilling the past into a few highly-visible events and ignoring false starts, mishaps, luck, and the actions of secondary players that likely had an impact on the outcome, they explain success and failure in a simple and digestible way. Most narratives are compelling only because they are coherent.

"Our comforting conviction that the world makes sense rests on a secure foundation: our almost unlimited ability to ignore our ignorance" (p. 201).

People ought to question the confidence they have in their understanding of the past because hindsight bias makes objective assessment of the past almost impossible. The present alters the perception of the past. Your mind is adept at revising the narrative in your head to accommodate and make sense of surprises. In hindsight, events that happened in the past seem as if they were certain to happen. When your mind acclimates to new information, you lose much of what you thought about the incident before it happened. In this way, you know less about the past than you think you do.

Chapter 20: The Illusion of Validity

System 1 and System 2 construct stories to make sense of reality. The confidence an individual has in his opinions, predictions, and beliefs simply reflects the coherence of the story he has in his mind and the ease with which he constructed it. Confronted with data that contradicts these opinions or predictions, he may accept it intellectually, but he will ignore it to maintain coherence and continue to act as if the story in his mind is still valid. In this way, confidence is a terrible metric for the validity of judgment.

Confidence can also arise out of the illusion of skill. The true measure of skill is consistency. If an investor, salesperson, or golfer is truly skilled, his year-to-year results should not vary erratically. If they do, years of exceptional performance are just lucky years. Intellectually, traders know their stock picks are, over the long run, no better than stocks picked at random. But years of studying and analyzing data combined with a professional culture that overstates skill, reinforces the illusion of skill.

Chapter 21: Intuitions vs. Formulas

Statistical predictions that use formulas with a few variables are significantly better at predicting outcomes—be they student grades or prognoses of cancer patients—than subjective assessments made by professionals. Experts make poorer predictions than algorithms because they consider complex combinations of variables, the result being more extreme predictions than if a few variables were considered. The inconsistency of human judgments, combined with the overconfidence professionals have in their intuition, also weakens the quality of subjective predictions.

Chapter 22: Expert Intuition: When Can We Trust It?

Intuition is an exercise in recognition. A situation provides a cue, and System 1 searches associative memory for similar or related situations and their solutions. If it finds something familiar, it gives a quick, intuitive judgment.

Recognition is reinforced by emotional experiences and prolonged exposure to cues. Emotional experiences (including fearful experiences) are easily stored as memories that support intuition. Prolonged practice—but only in a regular, predictable environment—helps develop reliable intuition.

Chapter 23: The Outside View

The planning fallacy is the tendency to expect ideal rather than realistic conditions when making plans. People often choose the coherence of the best case scenario over what seems like an implausible base rate—the average probability of success or time it takes to complete similar projects.

In their assessment of project longevity and success, people tend to search internal evidence—the circumstances of their inside view—and assume existing conditions will prevail or improve. They don't consider what may go wrong, or the unknown unknowns.

Chapter 24: The Engine of Capitalism

Optimistic bias leads people to neglect probabilities of success, overestimate their ability and level of control, and downplay the influence of luck and external conditions. This bias explains why entrepreneurs and investors take on unnecessary risk.

When businesspersons anchor on their plans, ignore the statistics of their industry, and neglect what they don't know, they take on avoidable risks and magnify their rate of failure.

"An unbiased appreciation of uncertainty is a cornerstone of rationality—but it is not what people and organizations want...Acting on pretended knowledge is often the preferred solution" (p. 263).

PART 4:
CHOICES

Chapter 25: Bernoulli's Errors

In 1738, Daniel Bernoulli pointed out that people dislike risk and prefer sure choices to gambles with higher expected value. He argued that people make choices based on utility (the psychological value of money) not on expected value, and considered that marginal utility diminishes with increasing wealth.

Bernoulli overlooked the fact that utility depends on changes in wealth, not on the value of current wealth, and on the reference point. How happy you are with your money depends on what you recently gained or lost, not what you have. It also depends on your reference point—the amount you had before the change.

Chapter 26: Prospect Theory

In prospect theory, gains and losses determine the value of options, and people assess these gains and losses using irrational rules of thumb. If an individual is given identical choices but one is framed in terms of gains and the other in terms of losses, he will choose the one framed as a gain and judge it as more valuable.

Prospect theory holds that people are instinctively loss averse. They respond more strongly to losses than gains of the same amount. They will take the sure thing when they stand to gain and prefer the risky choice where loss is involved.

Chapter 27: The Endowment Effect

People base their assessment of options on their reference point and endow the things or options they own with more significance than those they don't own. An individual may not care which of two similar options he gets. However, he will be unlikely to trade one gain for the other after owning it for some time. The gain he chose became his reference point when he made the choice. The disadvantage of losing the incumbent gain will weigh more strongly in his mind than the advantage of acquiring the second gain.

Ownership increases the perceived value of the goods people purchase for use. Selling something you would use—such a ticket to a sold-out event—usually registers as a painful transaction. Experienced traders find it easier to make the trade because they consider how much they want to have something relative to how much they want to keep what they have.

Chapter 28: Bad Events

The human mind prioritizes bad events. Both real and symbolic threats activate the amygdala—the brain's threat center—before the conscious registers the threat. This prioritization explains why people are more motivated to avoid loss than to acquire gains.

Chapter 29: The Fourfold Pattern

When you evaluate a complex object or event, System 1 automatically considers its constituent parts or outcomes and assigns more weight to some than others. The weighting may be different if the evaluation is the deliberate undertaking of System 2. Either way, improbable outcomes and small risks are given disproportionate weights up to a factor of four (which explains the appeal of insurance, despite hefty premiums).

People are risk averse in situations where there is a high probability of making gains and where there is a low probability of incurring loss (think insurance). In either case, they are likely to accept unfavorable settlements in exchange for certainty. On the other hand, they prefer to gamble where there is a low probability of making gains (think lotteries) and where there is a high probability of incurring loss—in the expectation they will avoid the loss. This is the fourfold pattern.

Chapter 30: Rare Events

People overestimate and, consequently, overweight the likelihood of rare events such as terrorism and natural disasters. The coverage of these events in the media elicits emotions that are easily accessible with the sighting of a cue. When you notice a cue that recalls the memory of the death and destruction you saw on the news, System 1 instinctively seeks ways to relief the fear the cue invokes. System 2 may know the risk is miniscule, but it can't override the uneasiness created by System 1.

Chapter 31: Risk Policies

System 1 automatically evaluates options and expresses preference for sure gains and non-sure losses before System 2 computes the expected values of the options. Most people go with the compelling impression made by System 1.

If you can broadly consider all the options you have and compute their value, you can mitigate the emotional reaction System 1 makes to loss, take favorable gambles, and reduce the inconsistency of your decisions.

Chapter 32: Keeping Score

For people above the poverty line, getting more money is not so much about affording a better life as is it about evening an internal score of achievement. In the mental account, gain registers as a pleasurable reward and loss as a painful punishment that creates a negative balance. People often make irrational decisions to even this mental account. Amateur investors, for example, close winners early to maintain a positive mental record and hold on to obvious losers in the hope they will turn around and even the score.

System 1 keeps this mental record of pleasure and pain and nudges you to maintain a good balance. It takes the deliberate mobilization of System 2 to rationally assess the economic value and future consequences of current decisions and to avoid the temptation to invest more in a losing gamble.

Chapter 33: Reversals

The decisions people make when they consider one option differ from those they make when there are two or more options. In situations where only one scenario is under consideration, System 1 automatically creates an impression that System 2 endorses to make a decision.

Preference reversal often occurs if people are in a position to compare two or more situations. Situations that present comparisons take mental effort. They mobilize System 2, which makes more rational decisions.

Chapter 34: Frames and Reality

System 1 reacts to the way situations are framed. It doesn't process a 90 percent survival rate as being the same as a 10 percent mortality rate. Instead, it makes a quick preference to the option framed in terms of survival.

Reframing options takes energy and effort. System 2 chooses to forgo the effort and endorses the impression created by System 1. In this sense, without realizing it, most of your decisions may be influenced by the way descriptions are framed rather than by their content.

PART 5:
TWO SELVES

Chapter 35: Two Selves

The human mind has an experiencing and a remembering self. The experiencing self is active at the present; it assesses current levels of pain or pleasure. The remembering self makes retrospective assessments of experiences. Memories are retained long after the experience ends, so the remembering self is stronger and dominant. It determines how you view your life, what you learn, and how you make future decisions. A bad ending to a good experience ruins the memory of the experience, not the experience itself, but it creates an unwillingness to repeat the experience.

The actual pain you experience is a factor of the intensity and the duration of the painful experiences. However, the way you remember the pain will be influenced by the average of the peak and the end level of pain. The duration of the pain is of little consequence on your retrospective assessment of the pain. If you endure evenly intense pain for a short period, you will have a less painful experience but a more unpleasant memory than if you endure the same level of pain for longer, but the pain wanes towards the end.

Chapter 36: Life as a Story

The remembering self stores memories as sketches of significant events. The human mind uses the presence or absence of significant events and the quality of the ending to judge the quality of experiences. The duration of experiences is seldom a consideration. Doubling length of pleasurable or painful moments has little effect on how they are remembered.

Chapter 37: Experienced Well-Being

Since the stories the remembering self creates are heavily influenced by the peak and the end, this self is unreliable in the assessment of well-being.

Well-being is better determined by an assessment of time spent doing pleasant work and feeling pleasant emotions—less the time spent doing unpleasant work and feeling low or indifferent—than by a global estimation of satisfaction from memory.

Chapter 38: Thinking About Life

When people are asked how satisfied they are with their lives, the answer they give is usually influenced by a small sample of the events that immediately come to mind. System 1 substitutes global analysis of well-being with an assessment of readily available data. People also tend to give too much weight to circumstances they focus on, even when these circumstances have little influence on well-being. Any objective measurement of well-being must consider the feelings of both selves.

"Adaptation to a new situation, whether good or bad, consists in large part of thinking less and less about it. In that sense, most long-term circumstances of life, including

paraplegia and marriage, are part-time states that one inhabits only when one attends to them" (p. 405).

KEY TAKEAWAYS

Key Takeaway: Two Systems drive human thoughts and actions.

The working of the human brain is best described by two fictitious systems: System 1 and System 2. System 1 is the source of the subconscious drives and beliefs that form gut reactions. It operates effortlessly, makes instant evaluations, and provides the impressions and feelings that System 2 acts on to make choices and plan action.

System 2 is deliberate and effortful. It rationalizes the impressions and feelings from System 1 and makes intentional judgments. System 2 is naturally lazy, so it often endorses the impressions of System 1, even when they are biased.

Take: Fast thinking is automatic and effortless. Slow thinking is deliberate and mentally exerting.

System 1 is in charge of routine, automatic assessments. It assesses the body and the environment for familiarity and safety—a survival mechanism inherited from early caveman days. It prizes the coherence, not the quality or completeness of information, and spurs action based on what feels or doesn't feel safe, familiar, or good.

System 2 is intentional and deliberate. It handles complex problems and tasks and makes more logical decisions. When it is engaged, pupils dilate, attention becomes limited, and the body expends more energy. Since thinking slow is mentally exerting, the brain avoids it when it can.

Key Takeaway: Overreliance on System 1 fosters irrationality and lazy thinking.

People who respond to intuition without much critical thought tend to be impatient and impulsive and often seek immediate gratification. People who question intuition and rely more on slow thinking to make judgment have more cognitive control and perform better on intelligence tests.

Key Takeaway: Hunger, self-control, and mental fatigue deplete System 2.

Situations that require you to suppress natural instincts, such as ignoring obvious distractions, exhaust System 2. They weaken self-control and make resisting subsequent temptations difficult. When System 2 is exhausted, you are likely to be easily provoked, to make impulse purchases, to neglect healthy habits, and to make more intuitive errors. Hunger and mentally tasking work, which require disproportionate levels of energy, have the same effect. Consuming glucose replenishes energy and mitigates the effects of System 2 depletion.

Key Takeaway: You can't be too sure of the reasons for your choices.

System 2 is not as much in charge as people would like to believe. A lot of the time, decisions are guided by the impressions System 1 gathers from the environment. System 1 makes a story out of the information it gets, and System 2 looks for evidence to defend the story.

If you are exposed to images of money, you are more likely to take actions that reflect self-reliance and become less involved with others. It's hard to believe this phenomenon applies to you because priming is automatic and outside your conscious awareness.

Key Takeaway: The human mind favors plausibility over probability, certainty over doubt.

The most coherent stories—the ones the human mind is most likely to believe—are the ones that are plausible, not necessarily probable. Detailed descriptions are more persuasive because they make for complete stories. However, by virtue of the additional elements they introduce, less probable. The brain struggles to process statistical facts, so it chooses to ignore them altogether.

One of the major tasks of System 2 is to question the impressions and suggestions made by System 1. However, because questioning takes more energy than accepting, System 2 often endorses the intuitions that feel certain.

Key Takeaway: Use individual cases, not statistics, to teach or spur action.

System 1 is hardly ever influenced by mere statistics, except where they confirm a stereotype. If you would have people take a threat more seriously, you would describe it in terms of individual cases, not statistics. When you say five out of every 100 people die of some preventable cause, the threat registers more vividly than if you said 5 percent of people succumb to the cause.

Key Takeaway: Causal thinking undermines ability to accurately evaluate random events.

The human mind is a perpetual pattern seeker. It makes sense out of reality by linking causes to outcomes and clustering patterns that seem related. In this way, it is bound to see patterns and make order out of situations that are truly random. If it detects a small hint of regularity in a random event, it immediately rejects the event as truly random.

Key Takeaway: Base rates make for better predictions than stereotype or similarity judgments.

System 1's intuitive guesses exaggerate the accuracy of information. Whenever you make a prediction, question the validity of the information you used. If the information you need to make a prediction is scanty or the evidence is weak, it is safer to rely on the averages of the class or category you are considering.

A baseline prediction, by averaging the variables of reference classes, gives an outside view that is a better prediction of how the project will turn out and how long it will take.

Key Takeaway: Mobilize System 2 to correct intuitive guesses.

It takes effort to assess the quality of the evidence you use to make a prediction. To predict the performance of a firm, for example, start with an intuitive guess, and then consider the average performance of the industry of the firm. An accurate prediction should be in between. If you have no useful evidence to adjust your prediction towards the mean, go with the mean. If you have evidence to make adjustments, consider the strength of the factors you considered and use the aggregate value you assign these factors to move towards or away from the mean. If your evidence is very strong, you will move 100% of the distance and settle on your initial prediction.

"The way to block errors that originate in System 1 is simple in principle: recognize the signs that you are in a cognitive minefield, slow down, and ask for reinforcement from System 2" (p. 417).

Key Takeaway: Extreme performance regresses to the mean over time, and that's all there is to it.

The human mind, always in search of causal explanations, is quick to explain why extreme performance deteriorates or improves over time. Most of these extreme events have no cause, just a statistical explanation. A business that almost collapsed last year is bound to do better this year, and an athlete who had an exceptional season is bound to do poorly on the subsequent season. What he feels or does is of little consequence.

Key Takeaway: Confidence reflects the coherence, not the accuracy of the story.

Confidence is a poor metric for judging the accuracy of judgments and predictions because it only reflects the ease with which the mind has made up a history.

A better way to judge the accuracy of predictions is to consider the average of the class or category. An accurate prediction should not be too far off.

Key Takeaway: An easily explainable past gives the illusion of an easily predictable future.

The ability to link patterns of the past and construct a coherent story makes people overconfident and fools them into thinking they can predict how the future will unfold. There is little place for luck in the way people understand past events. Because they don't accommodate it in the explanation of past events, they fallaciously neglect it in their prediction of the future.

When it comes to making predictions about an unknowable future, expert predictions are consistently no better than random predictions. Yet experts tend to be overconfident in their predictions, usually because they forget that knowledge of many things does not translate to knowledge of the future.

Key Takeaway: Simple algorithms do better than expert judgments in making predictions.

Professionals tend to overestimate their skills because they encounter numerous incidences that prove them right. They transfer this confidence to future predictions, in the making of which they rely overly on their impressions and undermine the value of simple variables. A checklist with a few impactful and independent dimensions or traits and a simple rating system is more trustworthy than a general human assessment, which is bound to be plagued by biases.

Key Takeaway: It takes practice in a stable, regular environment to acquire reliable intuition.

Regular, stable environments provide feedback to assess validity of predictions. An experienced firefighter has learned regularities of the environments in which he operates and can make quick and accurate intuitive guesses. The same cannot be said of a startup founder.

Key Takeaway: People are instinctively loss averse.

The emotional impact of loss and gain influences the evaluation of both financial and nonfinancial choices. System 1 makes stronger emotional responses to losses than gains. People will choose huge, probable losses over smaller, sure losses and small, sure gains over bigger, probable gains.

Negativity dominance explains loss aversion. People are more motivated to avoid loss and maintain the status quo than to acquire gain.

Key Takeaway: The remembering self dominates the experiencing self.

The human mind tends to confuse the memory of an event with its experience. Since the remembering self overrides the experiencing self, you can have 59 minutes of bliss and one minute of agony and remember the experience as mostly unpleasant.

Key Takeaway: The peak and the end influence the memory of experiences.

System 1 neglects the duration of experiences in its retrospective assessment of events.

Because it averages the peak and the end, the mind tends to prefer painful experiences that were longer but got better in the end to shorter, evenly painful experiences. Good experiences that end badly are often remembered negatively. In this sense, memory alone cannot be relied upon to assess the quality of past experiences or well-being. An objective analysis of the length and quality of experiences makes for a better assessment.

EDITORIAL REVIEW

In his book *Thinking, Fast and Slow*, Daniel Kahneman argues that two mental systems influence the way people think, assess options, choose, and select appropriate action. One system, which he calls System 1, is the source of the automatic feelings and beliefs that influence gut reactions. The other system, System 2, makes deliberate assessments of choices and problems and articulates rational judgments. Kahneman maintains that the heuristics and biases that stem from System 1 invariably influence choices. Better choices, he argues, can be made by mobilizing the effortful System 2, part of which is to question assumptions and automatic impressions.

Thinking, Fast and Slow is a compilation of decades of behavioral economics research that Kahneman made with his friend and longtime collaborator Amos Tversky. It explores the experiments Kahneman conducted with Tversky to reveal cognitive biases, explains the improved theory of decision making that won Kahneman a Nobel Prize, and concludes with his work on well-being and life satisfaction.

Kahneman hopes to discredit the economic school of thought that postulates that consumers are rational. He hopes that by illustrating the most common errors of judgments, he can invite the reader to question his thinking and make better and consistent choices. He cites experiment after experiment that illustrates common breakdowns in rationality to make a comprehensive and compelling argument for his case. In the end, his view of a flawed but malleable human mind is, quite possibly, beyond reproach.

ABOUT THE AUTHOR

Daniel Kahneman is an Israeli-American psychologist, author, and Nobel laureate. He is best known for prospect theory, which he developed with Amos Tversky in 1992, and his work on behavioral economics and the psychology of judgment and decision making. *Thinking, Fast and Slow*, which covers much of his work, is a major *New York Times* bestseller. Kahneman has coauthored several other books, including *Attention and Effort, Judgment Under Uncertainty,* and *Choices, Values, and Frames.*

THE END

If you enjoyed this summary, please leave an honest review on Amazon.com...it'd mean a lot to us!

If you haven't already, we encourage you to purchase a copy of the original book.

89197202R00024

Made in the USA
Columbia, SC
10 February 2018